FRANCIS FRITH'S
AROUND BRISTOL
PHOTOGRAPHIC MEMORIES

AROUND BRISTOL

PHOTOGRAPHIC MEMORIES

CLIVE HARDY

First published in the United Kingdom in 1999 by
The Francis Frith Collection®

Hardback edition 1999
ISBN 1-85937-050-0

Hardback reprinted 2001

Paperback edition 2001
ISBN 10: 1-85937-264-3 ISBN 13: 978-1-85937-264-7

Paperback reprinted 2003, 2004

Revised paperback edition 2006

British Library Cataloguing in Publication Data

Around Bristol Photographic Memories
Clive Hardy

The Francis Frith Collection®
Frith's Barn, Teffont,
Salisbury, Wiltshire SP3 5QP
Tel: +44 (0) 1722 716 376
Email: info@francisfrith.co.uk
www.francisfrith.com

Printed and bound in Great Britain

Front Cover: **BRISTOL**, *Queen's Road 1900* 45653at

Frontispiece: **CLIFTON**, *The Bridge 1887* 20164

*The colour-tinting is for illustrative purposes only, and is not intended to be
historically accurate*

AROUND BRISTOL
PHOTOGRAPHIC MEMORIES

CONTENTS

The Making of an Archive   8

Bristol From the Air   10

Bristol - An Introduction   12

Around the City   16

Gloucestershire County Map   54

Bristol Docks and Avonmouth   56

Clifton   70

Bristol Ordnance Survey Map   78

Around and About   80

Index   88

VOUCHER FOR FREE MOUNTED PRINT   93

THE MAKING OF AN ARCHIVE

FRANCIS FRITH, Victorian founder of the world-famous photographic archive, was a devout Quaker and a highly successful Victorian businessman. By 1860 he was already a multi-millionaire, having established and sold a wholesale grocery business in Liverpool. He had also made a series of pioneering photographic journeys to the Nile region. The images he returned with were the talk of London. An eminent modern historian has likened their impact on the population of the time to that on our own generation of the first photographs taken on the surface of the moon.

Frith had a passion for landscape, and was as equally inspired by the countryside of Britain as he was by the desert regions of the Nile. He resolved to set out on a new career and to use his skills with a camera. He established a business in Reigate as a specialist publisher of topographical photographs.

Frith lived in an era of immense and sometimes violent change. For the poor in the early part of Victoria's reign work was a drudge and the hours long, and ordinary people had precious little free time. Most had not travelled far beyond the boundaries of their own town or village. Mass tourism was in its infancy during the 1860s, but during the next decade the railway network and the establishment of Bank Holidays and half-Saturdays gradually made it possible for the working man and his family to enjoy holidays and to see a little more of the world. With characteristic business acumen, Francis Frith foresaw that these new tourists would enjoy having souvenirs to commemorate their days out. He began selling photo-souvenirs of seaside resorts and beauty spots, which the Victorian public pasted into treasured family albums.

Frith's aim was to photograph every town and village in Britain. For the next thirty years he travelled the country by train and by pony and trap, producing fine photographs of seaside resorts and beauty spots that were keenly bought by millions of Victorians.

THE RISE OF FRITH & CO

Each photograph was taken with tourism in mind, the small team of Frith photographers concentrating on busy shopping streets, beaches, seafronts, picturesque lanes and

villages. They also photographed buildings: the Victorian and Edwardian eras were times of huge building activity, and town halls, libraries, post offices, schools and technical colleges were springing up all over the country. They were invariably celebrated by a proud Victorian public, and photo souvenirs – visual records – published by F Frith & Co were sold in their hundreds of thousands. In addition, many new commercial buildings such as hotels, inns and pubs were photographed, often because their owners specifically commissioned Frith postcards or prints of them for re-sale or for publicity purposes.

In order to gain some understanding of the scale of Frith's business one only has to look at the catalogue issued by Frith & Co in 1886: it runs to some 670 pages. By 1890 Frith had created the greatest specialist photographic publishing company in the world, with over 2,000 stockists! The picture on the right shows the Frith & Co display board on the wall of the stockist at Ingleton in the Yorkshire Dales (left of window). Beautifully constructed with a mahogany frame and gilt inserts, it displayed a dozen scenes.

POSTCARD BONANZA

The ever-popular holiday postcard we know today took many years to appear, and F Frith & Co was in the vanguard of its development. Postcards soon became a hugely popular means of communication and sold in their millions. Frith's company took full advantage of this boom and soon became the major publisher of photographic view postcards.

Francis Frith died in 1898 at his villa in Cannes, his great project still growing. His sons Eustace and Cyril continued their father's monumental task, expanding the number of views offered to the public and recording more and more places in Britain, as the coasts and countryside were opened up to mass travel. The archive Frith created continued in business for another seventy years. By 1970 it contained over a third of a million pictures of 7,000 cities, towns and villages. The massive photographic record Frith has left to us stands as a living monument to a special and very remarkable man.

This book shows Bristol as it was photographed by this world-famous archive at various periods in its development over the past 150 years. Every photograph was taken for a specific commercial purpose, which explains why the selection may not show every aspect of the city landscape. However, the photographs, compiled from one of the world's most celebrated archives, provide an important and absorbing record of Bristol.

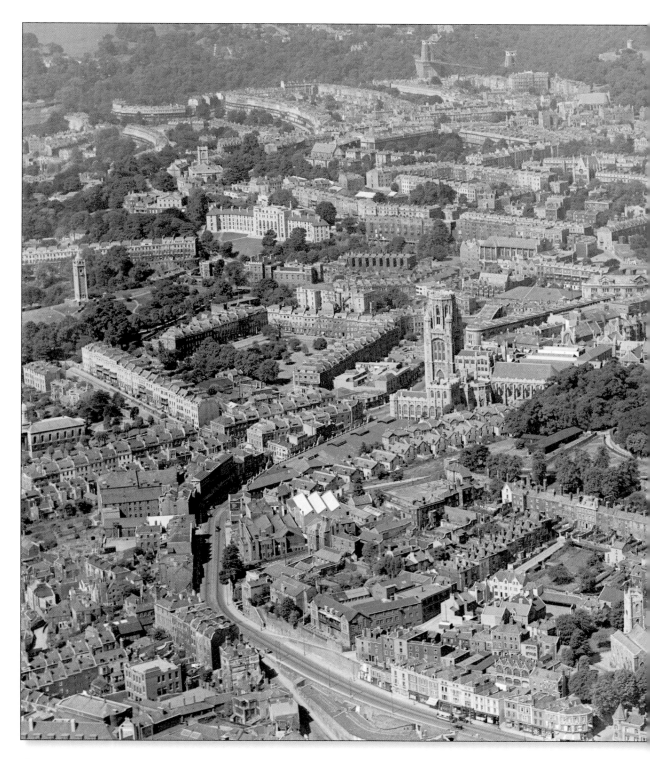

BRISTOL FROM THE AIR 1933 AF41484

BRISTOL - AN INTRODUCTION

THIS FAMOUS old city, situated seven miles up the Avon from the Bristol Channel, rose to become the second most important city in England after London. As early as the 10th century there was a mint, and in 1373 it was designated as a county in its own right. But it was the navigable Rivers Avon and Severn that gave Bristol its competitive edge; by the 12th century there was an established wine trade with the Bordeaux region, which was soon extended to Spain. In 1445 the Mariners' Guild was founded, and the Fellowship of Merchants was set up in 1500. In 1552 the Merchant Venturers were incorporated, and from then on sea-going Bristol ships could, theoretically, be found anywhere in the known world. Though most were involved in the trade with Spain, during the grain shortages of the 1580s several ships made trips to the Baltic.

During the Civil War, the possession of Bristol was vital to the King's cause. While the Royal Standard flew over the second most important city in England, the diplomatic initiatives to obtain foreign military assistance had currency. If it fell, then the King's cause would be seriously undermined. On 15 March 1643 Sir William Waller, with a force of fewer than 2,000 Parliamentary troops, had managed to secure the city, but the following July he was badly defeated at Roundway Down and his army was all but destroyed. Prince Rupert marched on Bristol, whose garrison had been stripped by Waller prior to his defeat, and summoned its defenders, under Colonel Nathaniel Fiennes, to surrender. Fiennes rejected the offer and two days later the Royalists attacked. Despite an outstanding defence, which inflicted heavy casualties on the Royalists, Fiennes had little hope of holding out and had no alternative but to ask for terms. Magnanimous in victory, Rupert allowed the garrison to march out of the city with the full honours of war: drums beating and flags flying. Despite his stand, Fiennes was tried the following August and condemned to death, though he was later reprieved.

Bristol now became the major Royalist base in the West Country for both land and naval operations, and a port for blockade runners bringing weapons and supplies from Europe. Mindful of Fiennes' difficulties in defending a city with a large perimeter, Prince Rupert set about strengthening the defences, which included the construction of the Royal Fort on Windmill Hill.

Following the battle of Marston Moor, Rupert returned to Bristol in October 1644 to organize defences and prepare for an expected siege; this came the following August, after the Royalist disaster at Naseby. Ordering the burning of Clifton, Bedminster and Westbury, Rupert pulled his forces into the city. Though Rupert wrote to the King promising to hold Bristol, his own combat experience must have told him that it was a hopeless cause. After putting up stiff resistance, the parleying for terms began on 4 September 1645, with the final surrender occurring on the 10th. With the loss of Bristol it could be argued that the war was lost.

PRIVATEERS AND SLAVERS

During the 18th century a large number of Bristol vessels undertook voyages as privateers. Sailing under letters of marque, a privateer was a privately armed vessel, authorized to wage war upon the king's enemies, in return for prize money. During the War of the Austrian Succession and the Seven Years War, the wet dock at Sea Mills was used as a privateer base. During the American War of Independence, 157 Bristol ships sailed under letters of marque, and during the French Revolution and the Napoleonic Wars, the city furnished a total of 63 privateers.

Not all the slaves handled by Bristol were from Africa. From the early years of the 17th century, thousands of men and women were sentenced by English courts to servitude in the colonies of the New World; the majority were destined to work on plantations. It was soon realized, however, that if the plantation system was to be maintained and expanded an alternative source of labour had to be found, and by 1619 the first cargoes of negro slaves were landed. Until the Restoration, slaving was carried on by English, Dutch and a few colonial ships, but the majority of merchants involved in the Guinea trade, as it was called, were more interested in gold and ivory than in human cargo.

Things changed in the 1660s with the establishment of the joint-stock Royal African Company. From now on, slaving would become the main traffic. The Royal African Company tried to maintain a monopoly on the slave trade, and though a few Bristol merchants held shares in it, most were for free trade, and were of the opinion that any competent captain could cruise the West African coast, slaving at will. And this is precisely what most of them did. Despite a petition from the Royal African Company, Parliament threw the slave trade open to anyone prepared to pay 10 per cent tax on a voyage. In 1707-08, of the 52 ships that cleared Bristol to take part in the Guinea trade, fifty were free traders. In 1725 Bristol cleared 63 ships with a total capacity for 16,950 slaves, and though twenty years later the number of ships had been reduced to 47, the carrying capacity had dropped by only 310 slaves.

Though Bristol and London controlled slaving, they were soon to be eclipsed by a new player, Liverpool. With a different pay structure in operation, Liverpool ships were more profitable per voyage than their rivals at London and Bristol. In 1753 Liverpool cleared 63 slavers, Bristol 27, London 13, Lancaster 7, Glasgow 4, Chester 1, and Plymouth 1. Between 1756 and 1786, a total of 588 slaving voyages were made from Bristol, while Liverpool vessels made 1,858.

The slavers did not always have it their own way. In 1759, a slave ship operating along the Gambia River was attacked and boarded by natives. The captain who was badly wounded, and seeing that his ship was about to be overrun, made his way to the powder magazine and fired his pistol into it. The ship blew up killing everyone on board.

In May 1750, the Bristol slaver 'King David' was overrun by slaves who had managed to break into the arms locker. The captain and five crewmen were killed, while the rest took refuge in the hold. The leader of the slaves, who spoke good English, told the surviving crewmen that if they came up on deck they would be spared, but as each man came topside he was put in irons and given Jonah's toss (thrown overboard). The mate was the last to come up, and was only spared when it was realized that there was no one else left who knew how to handle the ship or navigate.

Bristol continued to send ships to West Africa that were unconnected with the slave trade, but there were never many of them. In 1840, some of the ships clearing Bristol included 45 for the West Indies, 14 for Newfoundland, 14 for West Africa, 9 for Canada, 7 for Australia and 3 for the East Indies. In 1835, a cargo of tea was landed directly from Canton, but attempts to establish the Bristol Tea Co and offer an alternative port to London failed.

By the early decades of the 19th century, Bristol was suffering and losing out to London, Liverpool and Hull, owing to the high charges imposed by the dock company. In 1840, Bristol had at least seven ships operating on the route to Australia, but docking dues, which were seven times greater than that charged by Liverpool, killed the traffic. Exports to Australia remained, but on a small scale.

It was only in the 20th century that Bristol, thanks to the development of Avonmouth, managed to return to something like the bustling days of the 18th century. In 1890, it was selected as the UK port for the fortnightly Imperial West Indies mail service, and from 1921 liners from Rangoon and Colombo were making scheduled calls at Avonmouth. An important boost for Avonmouth came in 1901 when Elders & Fyffes inaugurated their fortnightly service to Port Limon, Costa Rica. For over sixty years the banana

ENTRANCE TO THE DOCKS 1900 45555

BRISTOL - AN INTRODUCTION

ships would use Avonmouth, which involved the railways in operating over 400 special banana trains a year. Following the completion of the Royal Edward Dock in 1908, Avonmouth continued to expand.

In 1911, twenty-seven oil storage tanks were installed near the docks, and an oil basin was added in 1919. Between 1922-23 the eastern arm of the Royal Edward was built, alongside which were constructed large transit sheds and granaries. In 1938 the docks handled 51 ships carrying 231,000 tons of fruit, oilseeds, rice and tea from India, Burma, Ceylon and Malaya, while a further 86 ships discharged over 200,000 tons of cargo from Australia and New Zealand. The total for the year was 354 ships with more than one million tons of cargo landed.

Matthew's Bristol Directory of 1828 states that 'Bristol is ranked the second city in England in respect of riches, trade and population'. Things were about to change. Industrialization would see obscure places like Middlesbrough, which had a population of less than fifty people, expand in less than one hundred years to a town of over 90,000 inhabitants. In 1700, Bristol's population was approximately 20,000 which would put it in third place behind London and Norwich. By 1800, with a population of 60,000, it had slipped to sixth place, and by 1850, with 137,000 inhabitants, it would be ranked seventh. In terms of being a port, Bristol was, in 1700, the second largest in England. By 1800 it had dropped to

eighth, but by 1855 had pulled back to sixth largest, but ranked twelfth in terms of overseas trade.

BY ROAD AND RAIL

By the beginning of the 19th century the Bristol Mail from London offered a fast service. The 105 miles from Hyde Park Corner to York House, on the outskirts of Bath, could be covered in just eleven hours. The coach was scheduled to arrive at York House at half-past seven in the morning; after a change of horses, it proceeded through Bath and on to the Bristol road. At the time, this section of road was considered to be the best in all of England, thanks to John Macadam. He had moved to Bristol around 1803, and later became surveyor to the Bristol Turnpike Trust. On crossing the Bristol Bridge, the coach continued up the High Street and then turned into Corn Street, where the post office was situated; the scheduled arrival time was four minutes past nine. Bristol had one of the busiest provincial post offices in the country. There were daily mails to London, Oxford, Birmingham and Portsmouth, as well as a Welsh mail and a West of England mail. The office was also responsible for the initial sorting of overseas mails to and from the Americas, Portugal and most Mediterranean ports. From the various inns in the city, such as the White Hart and the Bush, it has been estimated that over two hundred coaches arrived and departed daily.

St Augustine's Bridge 1901 47886

Bristol also had a considerable number of haulage firms operating scheduled services as far as Yorkshire and Nottinghamshire. The railways came to Bristol in 1835, with the opening of the southern section of the Bristol & Gloucester Railway, which involved the construction of the 515 yards long Staple Hill Tunnel. The Bristol terminus was at Avonside Wharf on the Floating Harbour. The second railway to enter the city was the Great Western, whose first train ran on the Bristol to Bath section on 31 August 1840. Ten trains operated on the first day, carrying nearly 6,000 passengers and generating revenue to the tune of £476. The line to London was completed in June 1840. The third railway was the Bristol & Exeter, with twelve Bristolians on the sixteen-strong board of directors, and Isambard Kingdom Brunel appointed as engineer. The line was worked with GWR locomotives and rolling stock, and when it opened throughout, in May 1844, it was the longest main-line in the country: the distance between London and Exeter was 194 miles.

CLIFTON SPA

As well as being a large, prosperous city and port, Bristol, or more accurately Clifton, developed as a spa; the Hotwells proved popular with high society, especially after the discovery of a second spring in 1702. During the 18th century, Clifton became a fashionable resort, and in this part of the country was second only to Bath. The resort had all the amenities one would expect: a pump room and assembly rooms were built in 1722, and even branches of some London shops would open there for the season.

When Thomas Newton was Bishop of Bristol, from 1761 to 1781, the Hotwells were popular with fashionable society, of which some members were Roman Catholic. England at that time was Protestant in all things, and those of the Catholic faith were legally proscribed against in many situations. On hearing that there was a plan to open a 'mass house' at the Hotwells, Bishop Newton called in Bristol's lone Catholic priest, Father Scudamore, for a friendly chat. Having taken government advice on the matter, Bishop Newton left the priest in no doubt whatsoever that if he went ahead, he would feel the full weight of the law.

In 1870 the Docks Committee ordered the demolition of most of the facilities, but even up to the outbreak of the Great War it was estimated that around 350 people a day went to take the waters. The well was finally closed owing to its being contaminated by river water, which was seeping into it. A couple of bore holes were drilled, the aim being to strike the spring further back where, it was hoped, it would be free from pollution, but the enterprise was unsuccessful.

In 1828 Isambard Kingdom Brunel was staying at Clifton for his health, spending much of his time on sketching expeditions along the Gorge. By coincidence, in October 1829 the Merchant Venturers advertised for plans to bridge the Gorge, since money had been left for the purpose by William Vick in 1752. Despite competition from experienced engineers such as Thomas Telford, one of young Isambard's sketches was selected. Brunel's original estimate had been £52,966, but by the time the final design was ready the price had gone up to £57,000. Vick's legacy would not be enough, and it would be August 1836 before the foundation stone was laid.

Brunel's steamships, 'Great Western' and 'Great Britain', were built at Bristol, though both were too big to be able to use the Floating Harbour. The 'Great Western', which pioneered transatlantic steamer services, was a wooden paddle-steamer of 1,340 tons, and though she was based at Kingroad near the mouth of the Avon, the money-grabbing Bristol Dock Co still demanded full port dues on her. The 'Great Britain', being a much larger vessel and built of iron, was immediately based at Liverpool, where she was joined by the 'Great Western' in 1842. Both ships drew large crowds when they were first towed out of Bristol and through the Gorge at Clifton.

KEYNSHAM

During the Monmouth Rebellion of 1685, the bridge over the Avon at Keynsham became vital to the strategic planning of both sides. If Monmouth could take it, he could attack Bristol, which was defended by the Duke of Beaufort who had a few militia units and some regulars at his disposal. If the king's forces could destroy the bridge, Monmouth would be held up for at least a couple of days while it was repaired, though he would still be in a position to attack Bristol before he could be engaged by the bulk of the royalist forces on their way to intercept him. Monmouth would also have had an opportunity to give the royalists the slip by heading for the North via Gloucester.

Left: ST MARY REDCLIFFE 1887 20153
As large as a cathedral and one of only two parish churches in England to have stone vaulting, St Mary's was built on a grand scale, thanks to the generosity of Bristol merchants. The interior is 275ft in length, 117ft across the transepts, and the spire is 292ft high.

Above: ST MARY REDCLIFFE, NORTH PORCH 1901 46502
The name Redcliffe derives from the red sandstone outcrop upon which the church stands. The church is built of oolitic limestone.

Left: ST MARY REDCLIFFE, THE NAVE 1887 20157
The stone vaulted nave, looking east. The church houses some interesting artefacts, including what is purported to be a rib from the Dun Cow, said to have been slain by that old-fashioned homicidal maniac, Guy of Warwick; it is, in fact, a whale-bone, thought to have been presented by Cabot.

Above: ST MARY REDCLIFFE, THE ALTAR 1887 20159
The magnificent St Mary Redcliffe owes much to the generosity of William Canynge the elder (died 1396), and his grandson William Canynge the younger (1394?-1474). In front of the high altar is a brass to John Brooke and his wife Johanna. She was the daughter of Richard Amerycke, collector for Customs and patron of John Cabot. So just who was America named after?

THE CABOT TOWER 1900 45564

In 1497 John Cabot, under the patronage of Richard Amerycke, sailed from Bristol in the ship 'Matthew'. On 24 June Cabot discovered mainland America, and the following year his son Sebastian explored the American coast from Newfoundland to Florida. A replica of John Cabot's tiny ship, the 'Matthew', was sailed to Newfoundland in 1999 to commemorate the voyages of the Cabots, and can now be seen at Bristol's Great Western dock.

THE STATUE OF JOHN CABOT 2005 B212712

AROUND THE CITY

The
Cathedral
1890 24634
The west towers
shortly after they had
been completed. The
Bristol dioceses was
created by Henry
VIII in 1542, and
comprised eighteen
parishes within the
city boundaries,
fourteen others in
Gloucestershire,
and Abbots Leigh
in Somerset. It was
refounded by Pope
Paul IV in 1557.

THE CATHEDRAL,
THE ELDER LADY CHAPEL
1900 45578
Bristol cathedral has two Lady Chapels. The Elder Lady Chapel was built by Abbot David around 1210-1215, and was restored in the 1890s. Originally it was detached from the main building, but was incorporated at some time between 1298 and 1363 when the choir was reconstructed.

THE CATHEDRAL 1887 20141
The bishopric was one of the poorest in England, and even in the mid 18th century its net revenues were only around £300 a year. Because of this, bishops were given additional church preferments. When Thomas Secker was appointed in 1735, he also held the prebend of Durham and the rectory of St James, Westminster. Even so, Secker found it hard to make ends meet.

THE CATHEDRAL, THE NAVE 1900 45572

Because it lacks a clerestory and triforium, the aisles rise to the same height as the nave, a feature making Bristol unique among English cathedrals. The original Norman nave was partially reconstructed at the time of the Dissolution, but then was allowed to fall into ruin. The present nave is 19th century and was built, along with the west towers, between 1868 and 1888.

THE CATHEDRAL, THE CHOIR
1900 45573
This photograph looks east toward the reredos
and the stone screen. The reredos was erected in
1899, and is renowned for its skeleton vaulting
and stellate tomb recesses.

THE CATHEDRAL, THE CHOIR, WEST 1900 45575
At this date, entry to the main body of the church was free, but the sub-sacrist kept the keys to the Chapter House (considered one of the
finest Norman chambers in the country), the Elder Lady Chapel and the Berkeley Chapel. The fee to see these gems was 6d.

AROUND THE CITY

Right: COLLEGE GREEN 1887 20128
Originally, College Green was the burial ground for the Augustinian abbey, founded by Robert Fitzhardinge in 1148, and for a hospital, founded jointly by Maurice Berkeley of Gaunt and his nephew, Robert de Gourney. Bristol also had two hospitals for lepers: St Mary Magdelene's, Brightbow, was for women, while a similar institution for men existed to the east of the town boundary.

Below: PARK STREET 1900 45654
It was along here that the Philosophical and Literary Institution had its premises in the early years of the 19th century, and one of the first scientific lecturers was Humphrey Davy. Davy also belonged to the Bristol Library Society. Its members included Samuel Taylor Coleridge, Robert Southey and William Wordsworth.

PARK STREET 1950 B212271

The Gothic tower of the university rises above the rooftops. Incorporated in 1909, the main university buildings were paid for by Sir George Arthur Wills and his brother Henry Herbert Wills in memory of their father.

PARK STREET 1900 45653
For decades a major problem facing the Bristol Health Board was how to combat the daily stench during the summer months created by tons of horse-droppings. An early experiment using water-carts to damp down the streets found that it took 7,000 gallons to water one mile of street, 18 feet in width, at a cost of 8s 4d per mile. The result of the 1861 experiment found that Bristol would need 83 carts to water the streets twice a day.

AROUND THE CITY

Left: THE UNIVERSITY FROM CABOT TOWER c1950 B212203
The university tower was designed by
Sir George Oatley, and completed in 1925. Sir George also
designed the physics laboratory at the Royal Fort, which was
opened by Lord Rutherford in 1927.

Below: QUEENS ROAD 1900 45653A
Queens Road, at the top of Park Street, was chosen as the
site for both the City Art Gallery and the City Museum.
As well as containing works by Gainsborough, Constable
and Reynolds, the Art Gallery is also home to Hogarth's
altarpiece from St Mary Redcliffe, and Solario's Withypool
Triptych, which is dated 1514.

ST AUGUSTINE'S BRIDGE 1900 45649
Barrow boys, porters and carters do their best to earn a few shillings. Note the large pair of spectacles above the optician's shop. Victorian retailers were fond of using such devices, which were usually painted gold, to advertise their premises.

BRISTOL, CITY CENTRE c1950 B212258
St Augustine's Parade was an interesting mix of architectural styles and advertisements. Whatever happened to Abdullah cigarettes?

AROUND THE CITY

PERO'S BRIDGE 2005 B212721
In 1999 Pero's Bridge was opened as
a memorial to those who had suffered
as a result of the slave trade, and in
recognition of the part they played in
the wealth of Bristol in the past.
It is named after Pero, who lived from
approximately 1753-1798, and who
was the slave of a rich Bristol merchant
called John Pinney

AROUND THE CITY

St Augustine's Bridge 1901 47886

Bristol's electric tramway system was inaugurated on 14 October 1895. This picture shows several cars at the terminus near to St Augustine's Bridge. The tramway was operated by a private company, rather than the Corporation, until 1937.

ST AUGUSTINE'S BRIDGE 1901 47885
The Tramways Act of 1870 gave powers to Bristol Corporation to take over the system at book price in 1915, or at any seventh year thereafter. Every seven years the council could not get its act together to make a firm commitment. The result was that the tramway company spent very little on upgrading the system, and it remained virtually unaltered throughout its forty-six year existence.

Above: CITY CENTRE
1950 B212227
St Augustine's Bridge looks
pretty much the same as it did
at the beginning of the 20th
century, though the trees have
grown, the trams have gone, and
there is neither a horse nor a pile
of horse muck in sight.

Right: THE CENTRE
C1950 B212255
St Augustine's Parade is just out
of sight on the left, and Broad
Quay is seen on the right. The
area is known locally as 'The
Scilly Isles'. These gardens were
created in 1938 when the Frome
from St Augustine's bridge was
culverted.

THE CENTRE c1953 B212283
The crown was made as part of the decorations for the coronation of Queen Elizabeth II, and was sold to Canada after the celebrations.

THE CENTRE c1950 B212265
The half-timbered building on the left is being used by Bristol bus and coach services. The Bristol Tramways and Carriage Co was taken over by the Corporation in 1937. All 237 trams were identical, and all were open-topped. The tramway closed in April 1941 when a bomb destroyed the power supply.

Opposite: THE CORN EXCHANGE, CORN STREET
2005 B212701

Left: ONE OF THE PILLARS ('NAILS') OUTSIDE
THE CORN EXCHANGE, CORN STREET
2005 B212708

'Paying on the nail' - the brass pillars, or nails, in
Corn Street, outside what used to be the Bristol Corn
Exchange, were used by merchants when striking a
bargain. The money was paid on the nail head, hence the
phrase 'to pay on the nail'.

BROAD STREET C1950 B212196

When Celia Fiennes visited Bristol in 1698 she noted that there were nineteen parish churches. There was no official place of worship for Catholics until the 1730s, and even then it was only created out of necessity. Abraham Darby owned a brassworks in the city, but in order to beat off foreign competition he needed to employ skilled Flemish workers; they would only come to Bristol if they were allowed to worship freely as Catholics.

Opposite: OLD HOUSES AND TOLLEY'S BANK 1890 24641
The junction of Wine Street and High Street. High Street was where Joseph Cottle opened a bookshop and publishing house in 1791. His authors included Samuel Taylor Coleridge and the local poet Robert Southey, who was born in Wine Street in 1774.

Right: THE BRIDGE 1901 47883
Looking across Bristol Bridge towards High Street. Dominating the picture is the church of St Nicholas. Bishop Secker's Diocese Book has an interesting comment on the church wardens. Abel Edwards was a profane swearer, blasphemer and drunkard, and John Veal lived in sin with Deborah Orstand. Thomas Williams and George Barrat appear to have kept bawdy houses.

Above: THE VICTORIA ROOMS C1950 B212253
Designed by Charles Dyer, the Victoria Rooms were built between 1838 and 1842. It was here, in June 1874, that a meeting was held to thrash out proposals whereby a university college might be established in the city. The college opened in 1876 in two houses in Park Row with just 87 day students and 234 evening students.

CHRISTMAS STEPS C1950 B212263

It was at the top of the Steps that John Foster founded an almshouse and chapel in 1481. The chapel, which was heavily restored in the 1880s, has an unusual dedication to the Three Kings of Cologne.

Above: CHRISTMAS STEPS
c1950 B212193

Christmas Steps are just behind Quay Street, and are thought to have been built in the 1660s. When this picture was taken, the Steps had long enjoyed a reputation as the place to go for antiques or to seek out old books.

Right: CHRISTMAS STREET
c1950 B212294

By the 1530s the old hospital of St Bartholomew had seen better days, and the decision was taken to convert it into a grammar school. The buildings and lands were eventually made over to the Corporation who were to act as governors. But Corporations being what they are, the lands were sold off and the school suffered accordingly.

BROADMEAD C1952 B212286
Here we see a mixture of Georgian, Victorian, thirties' style cinema, and postwar reconstruction.

BROADMEAD C1965 B212322
Broadmead runs between Union Street and Penn Street, and was a part of the regeneration of the city centre following the destruction of the Second World War. Redevelopment entailed the demolition of some of Bristol's older buildings, including the Ebenezer Chapel of 1795, and the extension of Broadmead to incorporate Rosemary Street.

YE LLANDOGER TROW
C1950 B212275
King Street still retains
many 17th and 18th
century buildings, despite
attempts by the Luftwaffe
to destroy them. Here we
see the Llandoger Trow Inn,
whilst a little way down the
street is the Theatre Royal,
home of the Bristol Old Vic
since 1946.

THE OLD THEATRE 1890 24640
The Theatre Royal opened in 1766 and was modelled on Christopher Wren's Drury Lane Theatre in London. Also to be found in King Street in 1890 were the St Nicholas Almshouse, founded in 1656, complete with its own chapel, and the Merchant Adventurer's Almshouses, built in 1699. The latter was restored following damage sustained during the Blitz; St Nicholas' was extensively restored in the early 1960s.

MERCHANT STREET C1965 B212324
Merchant Street following its redevelopment. The street was extended northwards so as to absorb Old King Street.

UNION STREET C1965 B212326
It was to this street, in 1793, that Joseph Storrs Fry moved his chocolate-making business. The business was founded by Joseph's father, who had come to Bristol from Wiltshire. Joseph Fry Senior had been involved in a number of business ventures and partnerships, but as a Quaker, the manufacture of chocolate was especially important to him, as it was a temperance drink.

St Peter's Hospital 1901 46499

In 1712 St Peter's Hospital looked after around three hundred sick and poor people. It was under the management of the Bristol Corporation for the Poor. Times were hard and the Corporation petitioned Parliament for permission to increase the rates. To support their cause they even commissioned a census.

ROYAL VICTORIA CONVALESCENT HOME 1901 46498

One of Bristol's more flamboyant characters was Richard Smith, chief surgeon at the Royal Infirmary, and a councillor from 1835 to 1843. His hobby was to write a rhyme relating to the career of every local criminal who had been executed and then sent to him for dissection. He would then bind the pages in the skin of the unfortunate felon.

MULLER'S NO 3 ORPHAN HOUSE 1901 46496

Prussian-born George Muller arrived in Bristol in 1833 and three years later started building five orphanages on this site at Ashley Down. As well as being a philanthropist, George was also a pastor with the Open Brethren and undertook preaching tours throughout the world. He died in 1892 at the ripe old age of ninety-two.

Left: TEMPLE CHURCH 1887 20129

In 1115, Hugue de Payens and Godfrey de Saint Adhemar founded a small group of Christian knights dedicated to the protection of pilgrims making the journey between Jericho and Jerusalem. The group was known as the Poor Knights of Christ, but it would later become the powerful Knights Templar. A small preceptory was established at Bristol during the late 12th century, and when the Order was suppressed in the 14th century the Temple Church, seen here in 1887, became the Holy Cross parish church.

Below: GENERAL VIEW 1900 45563

A view over the rooftops of Bristol. To the right of the cathedral can be seen something of the warehouses and wharves of the city docks. In the centre of the picture, to the left of the church spire, is one of the cone-shaped furnaces of a glassworks, somewhat akin to the bottlekilns of the Potteries. In 1793 Bristol had at least a dozen glassworks, producing a wide variety of glass and bottles for customers throughout the West Country.

AROUND THE CITY

THE CEMETERY 1887 20139

Opened in 1836 by the Bristol General Cemetery Co, Arnos Vale became the city's main burial ground until augmented by the opening of Greenbank Cemetery during the 1870s. Arnos Vale was laid out in terraces, and Charles Underwood designed its Doric lodges and classical chapels.

VIEW FROM BRANDON HILL 1896 38168

At various times between 1795 and 1840 the Corporation banned the use of the Guildhall for any type of meeting they considered to be Radical. As Bristolians had enjoyed free access rights to Brandon Hill since the 16th century, the Radicals simply held their meetings there, attracting large crowds; they were almost impossible to police.

EASTVILLE BOATING LAKES c1950 B212293

Leisure time within the city, though it is unlikely that the Frith cameraman would have hung around long enough to see if the fish were biting. This is one of a series of photographs taken by Frith for possible use as a postcard.

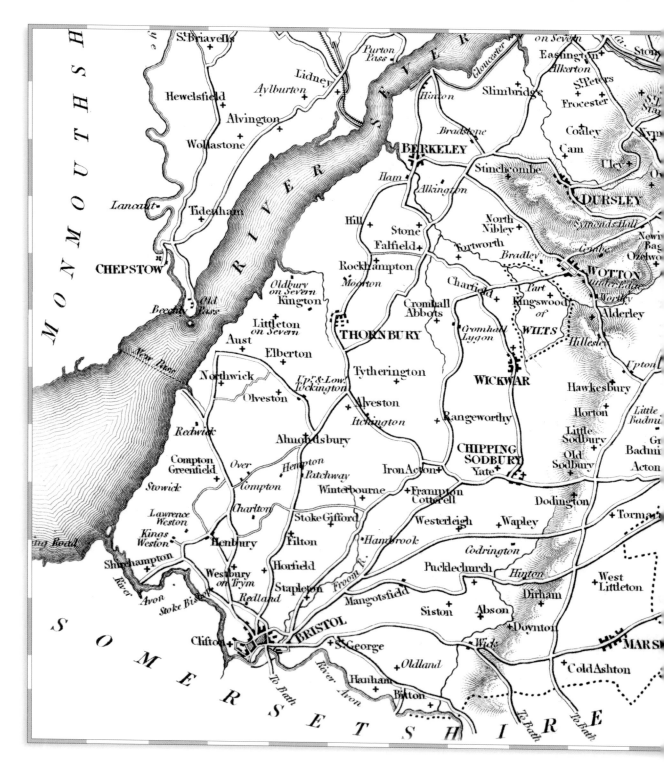

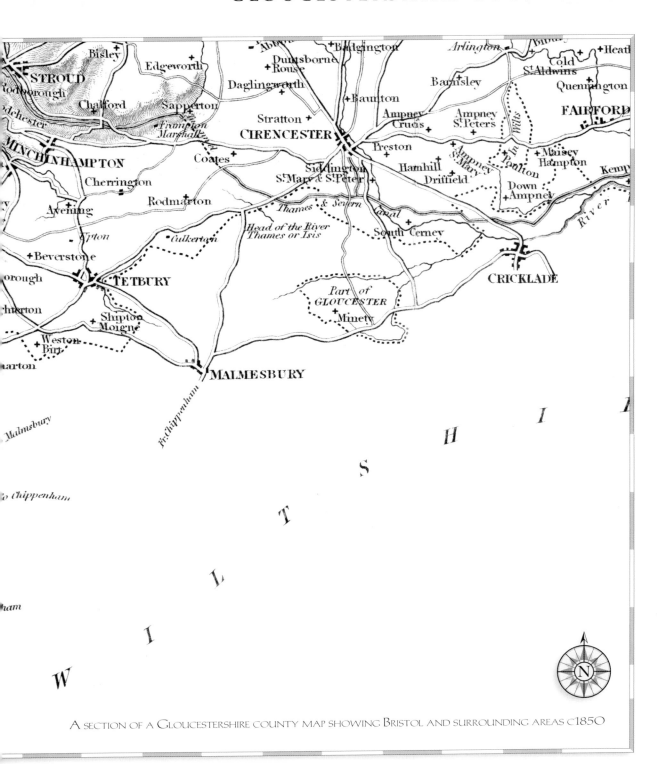

A section of a Gloucestershire county map showing Bristol and surrounding areas c1850

BRISTOL DOCKS AND AVONMOUTH

Above: EASTVILLE BOATING
LAKES c1950 B212288
From the same sequence as the previous
photo, and once again taken with a
view to being published as a postcard.

Left: FISHPONDS MEMORIAL
PARK c1950 B212291
A small boy rattles along the pathway
on his tricycle while older members of
the community seek shelter from the
sun. Once again this picture was taken
for possible publication in the Frith
postcard range.

BRISTOL DOCKS AND AVONMOUTH

ENTRANCE TO THE DOCKS C1950 B212186
The entrance lock to the Floating Harbour. In 1801-02 engineer William Jessop came up with his own designs for a tide-free city dock area that would enclose the Avon from Rownham to St Philip's. The river itself would be diverted by means of a New Cut from Totterdown to the entrance of the Floating Harbour. The project was completed by 1809, at a cost of about £600,000, with French prisoners of war being used for much of the manual labour.

BRISTOL DOCKS AND AVONMOUTH

ENTRANCE TO THE DOCKS 1900 45555

Even at this late date there were people advocating the 'dockisation' of the Avon, which would have resulted in the destruction of much of the natural beauty of the Gorge and the wholesale removal of Horseshoe Bend so that larger vessels could come up to the city. We may be thankful that it was decided that the facilities at Avonmouth should be extended instead.

BRISTOL DOCKS AND AVONMOUTH

Right: CLIFTON, THE SUSPENSION BRIDGE 1887 20167

A paddle tug prepares to get under way again after bringing a vessel up the Avon. The tugs greatly improved the ship-handling capabilities of the City Docks, and were far more efficient than the old rowed towboats.

Below: THE CENTRE c1950 B212266

A view from the Centre towards St Augustine's Reach. The Reach dates from the 13th century and used to extend further into the town. When it was built in 1248 it was an outstanding piece of civil engineering for its time, as it involved the diverting of the River Frome from its junction with the Avon at Bristol Bridge. The Reach established Bristol as the major port on the west coast.

Above: THE HARBOUR C1950 B212181

The City Docks. In the days of sail, vessels making their way up the Avon to Bristol had to contend with several problems: the current, the wind through the Gorge, and the serpentine course of the river itself. Vessels were assisted by towboats usually manned by ten or more rowers, and depending on the size of the ship and the prevailing conditions, anything up to ten towboats might be needed. In the 1770s the cost of bringing even a small vessel up the river from Pill could cost in the region of £10.

Right: THE DOCKS C1950 B212220

In 1823 the Chamber of Commerce were so concerned about the high cost of the port dues being demanded by the Bristol Dock Co that they inquired as to what charges would be levied at other ports for the same cargoes. At Bristol the dues would be £515,608, at Liverpool £231,800, at London £210,098 and at Hull £147,587. No wonder the port was losing trade.

BRISTOL DOCKS AND AVONMOUTH

VIEW FROM THE GRANARY 1901 47880

In 1897 the Dominion Line began a weekly scheduled service between Bristol and Canada, with the result that the importation of grain through the docks expanded. In that year the 'Montcalm' arrived at Avonmouth carrying over 6,000 tons of grain, which was the largest bulk cargo the docks had then handled.

BRISTOL DOCKS AND AVONMOUTH

THE DOCKS 1953 B212278

During the early decades of the 19th century, Bristol was losing trade to Hull, Liverpool, London and the South Wales ports owing to high dock charges. In 1833 the cost to discharge sugar and tobacco at Bristol was double that of Liverpool. By the mid 1840s it was cheaper to discharge goods at Liverpool, and then transport them by rail to Bristol, than it was to discharge them at the Bristol docks.

Above: THE DOCKS 1953 B212281
In the 1870s a railway line was built to serve the city docks. Though it was less than one mile long, it was expensive to build, requiring three bridges, a viaduct and a 282 yard-long tunnel under a burial ground, the cutting of which entailed the digging up of numerous former residents of Bristol and reburying them in a new cemetery at Brislington.

Right: THE NEW BASCULE BRIDGE c1950 B212243
Today the speed limit within the Floating Harbour is 6mph, and craft proceeding under the Prince Street, Redcliffe or Bristol Bridges should sound one prolonged blast on their horn before doing so.

THE QUAY 1887 20133

This photograph was taken three years after Avonmouth, Portishead and the city docks were brought under Corporation control. Bristol's two principal shipping companies were the Bristol Steam Navigation, founded in 1836 to take advantage of the Irish trade, and the Bristol City Lines, who were both owners and builders, with routes to South America and the East.

BRISTOL DOCKS AND AVONMOUTH

Above: AVONMOUTH DOCKS 1901 46494
The earliest scheme for a non-tidal basin at Avonmouth capable of taking vessels too large to reach Bristol was a £1.5 million project promoted in 1852. Alas, it got nowhere, but work did begin in 1868 on a single basin. After running into financial difficulties on several occasions, it eventually opened in 1877. While this was going on a rival scheme was being promoted at Portishead.

Left: AVONMOUTH DOCKS 1901 46493
In 1900 it was decided that the cargo handling and berthing facilities at Avonmouth needed upgrading so that the larger steamers then being built could use the port. Work began in 1902 on a new basin, and it was opened by King Edward VII in July 1908. The Royal Edward dock had a water area of 25 acres and a graving dock 875ft in length.

CLIFTON, THE SUSPENSION BRIDGE C1950 C120189

In 1752, William Vick bequeathed money towards the eventual bridging of the Gorge. It was not until 1829 that a competition was held for engineers and architects to submit designs. Despite entries from the likes of Thomas Telford, the competition was won by the still relatively inexperienced Isambard Kingdom Brunel.

CLIFTON

THE SUSPENSION BRIDGE
1887 20164

By 1843 work on the bridge had
ground to a halt, and the kitty was
empty; all the available money had been
used up on building the abutments. It
was not until 1864 that the bridge was
finally completed. The chains used to
support the road were bought second
hand, having been used on the old
Hungerford Bridge in London.

CLIFTON

Above: CLIFTON, THE SUSPENSION BRIDGE
1887 20168
The bridge has a total length of 1,352ft, while the distance
between the piers is 702ft. It is 31ft wide and the roadway
is 245ft above the high water level, so there is little chance
of a ship colliding with it.

Left: CLIFTON, LEIGH WOODS 1887 20175
The view from the suspension bridge towards Leigh
Woods. The railway line on the left is the single track
Bristol & Portishead Pier & Railway which was acquired
by the Great Western Railway in 1884, having been
converted to standard gauge in January 1880.

VIEW FROM CLIFTON BRIDGE C1965 B212312
The view from the suspension bridge looking toward the entrance lock to the Floating Harbour, and the junction lock of the New Cut and the Cumberland Basin.

CLIFTON, THE SUSPENSION BRIDGE 1897 38157
Bristol is where Brunel's steamships 'Great Western' and 'Great Britain' were built, though both were too big to use the Floating Harbour. Both ships drew large crowds when they were first towed out of Bristol and through the Gorge.

CLIFTON

CLIFTON, GRANBY HILL AND ST VINCENT'S PARK 1887 20162
As Clifton's reputation as a resort grew, the late Georgian terraces were built in a style that deliberately imitated Bath. Using Bath stone for the facings, the whole scheme was topped off with a series of splendid crescents offering superb views of the Gorge and surrounding countryside.

CLIFTON, THE COLLEGE 1887 20179

Clifton College became the most famous of all Bristol's schools. Founded in 1860 and opened in 1862, Charles Hanson designed the original buildings, including the Great Hall. The school's first headmaster, John Percival, is acknowledged as being responsible for making Clifton one of the leading schools of the day.

CLIFTON, THE COLLEGE 1901 46503

The college admitted both boarders and town boys, and somewhat uniquely for the period, regarded them all with equal status. Clifton was one of the first schools to teach engineering, and under headmaster James Wilson (1879-1890) the teaching of science was greatly improved.

CLIFTON, FROM THE DOWNS 1896 38165

Here we see the roofs of Clifton from the pleasantly wooded Downs. The Downs became as important to the resort as were the Hotwells; a favourite haunt for artists and visitors interested in the geology, flora and fauna of the area.

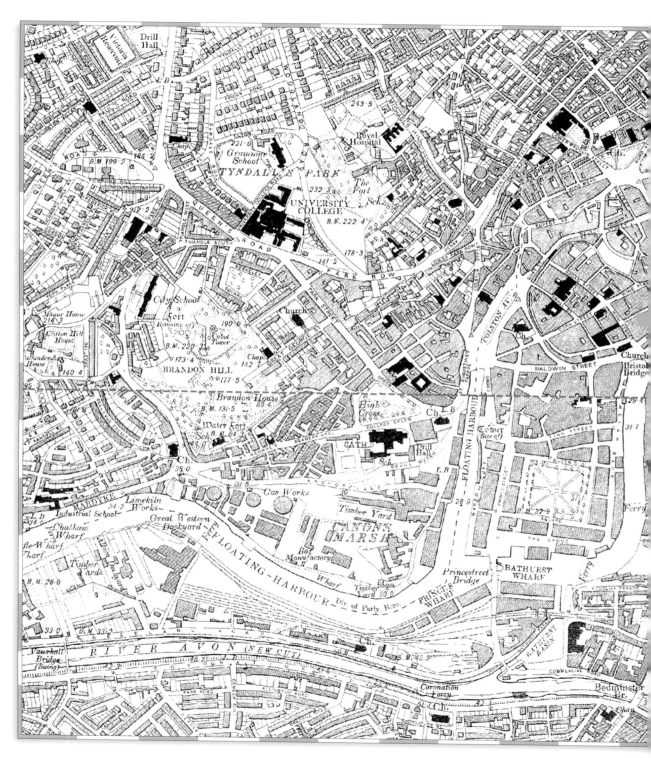

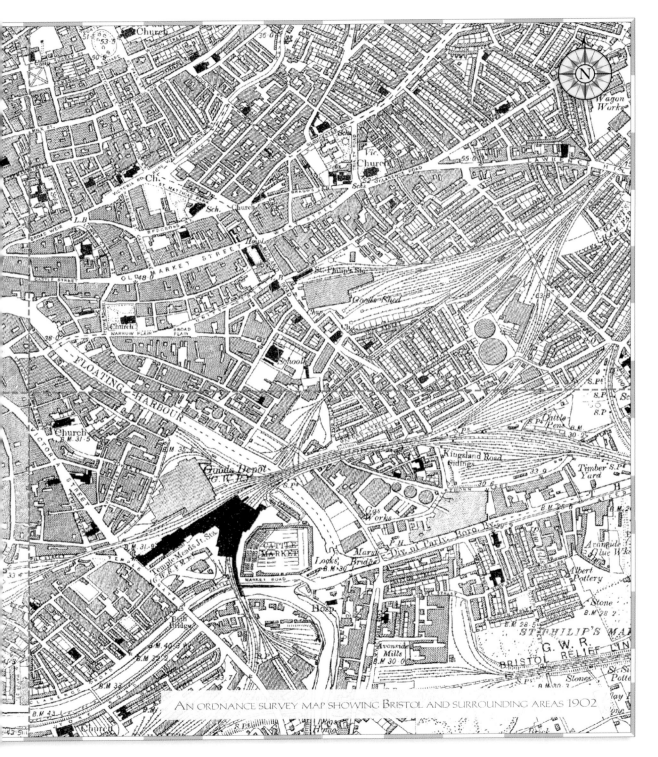

An ordnance survey map showing Bristol and surrounding areas 1902

AROUND AND ABOUT

THE ZOO C1960 B212311
Bristol Zoo has its home in Clifton and was founded in 1835.

KEYNSHAM, HIGH STREET 1950 K64003
On 26 June 1685 the village was the scene of a skirmish between 350 royalist troops and rebel forces of the Duke of Monmouth. Monmouth lost his nerve and turned away from Bristol. On arriving at Bath, Monmouth sent a messenger to the town to demand the surrender of the local garrison. The town's answer was to shoot the messenger dead.

HENBURY, BLAISE CASTLE C1955 H164303

Blaise Castle was built as a folly by Thomas Farr, Master of the Society of Merchant Venturers. In 1765 Thomas had been a member of a delegation sent by the Merchant Venturers to deliver a petition against the renewal of the Sugar Act; the government intended to use it to make the American colonies pay for their own defence. The merchants' close links with the Americans made them realize the Act would harm relations and damage trade. They were right.

AROUND AND ABOUT

HENBURY, THE POST OFFICE C1955 H164001
The Blaise Inn receives a pre-summer season coat of paint. The George Brewery was established in 1702, and was owned and run by the George family from 1788 until 1961 when it was bought by Courage. Now a part of Scottish Courage, Georges' Bitter Ale is still on sale, though it is unusual to find it outside the West Country or Southeast Wales.

HENBURY C1955 H164006
Nearby is Blaise Castle House which even in the 1920s had the best golf course in the area; green fees were 3s, Sunday play was available, and members of the ladies golf union were permitted. On the right of the picture is the village post office and shop.

SHIREHAMPTON, THE GEORGE INN c1955 S270004

Shirehampton is situated between Bristol and Avonmouth. In 1865 the Bristol Port & Pier Railway opened its single line between Avonmouth and Hotwells with intermediate stations at Sea Mills and Shirehampton. As this was a purely local railway, no provision had been made to connect it with any other railway. Even the opening date was kept a secret until a few minutes before the departure of the first train, for fear that the train would be overloaded; the railway only had one engine.

AROUND AND ABOUT

Above: SHIREHAMPTON, HIGH STREET c1955 S270001

Shirehampton was eventually linked by rail to Bristol with the opening of the Clifton Extension Railway in the 1870s. With the opening of Avonmouth Docks the line soon became very busy and had to be doubled in order to cope with the traffic.

Opposite Top: ALMONDSBURY, THE BOWL INN c1955 A103005

The Bowl Inn, when Georges' Beers was still a family run brewery. Scottish Courage's Bristol brewery is said to be the largest in the UK now dedicated to the brewing of real ale.

Opposite Bottom: ALMONDSBURY, THE VILLAGE c1955 A103001

As can be seen here, roads in the mid-1950s were a lot quieter than they are today. In 1955 UK car production reached a new record of nearly 900,000 cars and home sales were counted at over 500,000. Suddenly in November the Chancellor increased the purchase tax on new cars by 50 to 60 per cent in order to suppress the growing demand.

AROUND AND ABOUT

PORTISHEAD, THE ESPLANADE 1924 76002

The Bristol & Portishead Pier & Railway was a single broad-gauge line, which opened in April 1867, and connected with the Bristol & Exeter Railway at Bedminster. The pier opened in June 1868 and was soon extended so vessels could use it at low water. From Portishead there was a year-round steamer service to Cardiff and Newport and summer sailings to Ilfracombe.

INDEX

Almondsbury 85

Avonmouth Docks 68

Bascule Bridge 65

Blaise Castle 81

Bridge 43

Bristol Cathedral 22, 23, 24, 25

Broad Street 41

Broadmead 46

Cabot Tower 20

Cemetery 52

The Centre 60

Christmas Steps 44, 45

Christmas Street 45

City Centre 31, 38, 39

Clifton 76-77

Clifton College 75

Clifton Suspension Bridge 60, 69, 70-71, 72, 73

College Green 26

Corn Exchange 40, 41

Docks 13, 57, 58-59, 61, 62-63, 64, 65

Eastville Boating Lake 53, 56

Fishponds Memorial Park 56

Granby Hill 74

Harbour 61

Henbury 81, 82

John Cabot Statue 22

Keynsham 80

Leigh Woods 72

Merchant Street 48

Muller's Orphan Houses 50

'Nail' 41

Old Theatre 47

Park Street 26, 27, 28-29

Pero's Bridge 32-33

Portishead 86-87

Quay 66-67

Queen's Road 30

Royal Victoria Convalescent Home 50

Shirehampton 83, 84

St Augustine's Bridge 14, 31, 34-35, 36-37

St Mary Redcliffe Church 16-17, 18-19

St Peter's Hospital 49

Temple Church 51

Tolley's Bank 42

Union Street 48

University 30

Victoria Rooms 43

Ye Llandoger Trow 47

Zoo 80

The Francis Frith Collection Titles

www.francisfrith.com

The Francis Frith Collection publishes over 100 new titles each year. A selection of those currently available is listed below. For the latest catalogue please contact The Francis Frith Collection.

Town Books 96 pages, approximately 75 photos. **County and Themed Books** 128 pages, approximately 135 photos (unless specified). Pocket Albums are miniature editions of Frith local history books 128 pages, approximately 95 photos.

Accrington Old and New
Alderley Edge and Wilmslow
Amersham, Chesham and Rickmansworth
Andover
Around Abergavenny
Around Alton
Aylesbury
Barnstaple
Bedford
Bedfordshire
Berkshire Living Memories
Berkshire Pocket Album
Blackpool Pocket Album
Bognor Regis
Bournemouth
Bradford
Bridgend
Bridport
Brighton and Hove
Bristol
Buckinghamshire
Calne Living Memories
Camberley Pocket Album
Canterbury Cathedral
Cardiff Old and New
Chatham and the Medway Towns
Chelmsford
Chepstow Then and Now
Cheshire
Cheshire Living Memories
Chester
Chesterfield
Chigwell
Christchurch
Churches of East Cornwall
Clevedon
Clitheroe
Corby Living Memories
Cornish Coast
Cornwall Living Memories
Cotswold Living Memories
Cotswold Pocket Album
Coulsdon, Chipstead and Woodmanstern
County Durham
Cromer, Sheringham and Holt
Dartmoor Pocket Album
Derby
Derbyshire
Derbyshire Living Memories
Devon
Devon Churches
Dorchester

Dorset Coast Pocket Album
Dorset Living Memories
Dorset Villages
Down the Dart
Down the Severn
Down the Thames
Dunmow, Thaxted and Finchingfield
Durham
East Anglia Pocket Album
East Devon
East Grinstead
Edinburgh
Ely and The Fens
Essex Pocket Album
Essex Second Selection
Essex: The London Boroughs
Exeter
Exmoor
Falmouth
Farnborough, Fleet and Aldershot
Folkestone
Frome
Furness and Cartmel Peninsulas
Glamorgan
Glasgow
Glastonbury
Gloucester
Gloucestershire
Greater Manchester
Guildford
Hailsham
Hampshire
Harrogate
Hastings and Bexhill
Haywards Heath Living Memories
Heads of the Valleys
Heart of Lancashire Pocket Album
Helston
Herefordshire
Horsham
Humberside Pocket Album
Huntingdon, St Neots and St Ives
Hythe, Romney Marsh and Ashford
Ilfracombe
Ipswich Pocket Album
Isle of Wight
Isle of Wight Living Memories
King's Lynn
Kingston upon Thames
Lake District Pocket Album
Lancashire Living Memories
Lancashire Villages

Available from your local bookshop or from the publisher

The Francis Frith Collection Titles (continued)

Lancaster, Morecambe and Heysham Pocket Album
Leeds Pocket Album
Leicester
Leicestershire
Lincolnshire Living Memoires
Lincolnshire Pocket Album
Liverpool and Merseyside
London Pocket Album
Ludlow
Maidenhead
Maidstone
Malmesbury
Manchester Pocket Album
Marlborough
Matlock
Merseyside Living Memories
Nantwich and Crewe
New Forest
Newbury Living Memories
Newquay to St Ives
North Devon Living Memories
North London
North Wales
North Yorkshire
Northamptonshire
Northumberland
Northwich
Nottingham
Nottinghamshire Pocket Album
Oakham
Odiham Then and Now
Oxford Pocket Album
Oxfordshire
Padstow
Pembrokeshire
Penzance
Petersfield Then and Now
Plymouth
Poole and Sandbanks
Preston Pocket Album
Ramsgate Old and New
Reading Pocket Album
Redditch Living Memories
Redhill to Reigate
Richmond
Ringwood
Rochdale
Romford Pocket Album
Salisbury Pocket Album
Scotland
Scottish Castles
Sevenoaks and Tonbridge
Sheffield and South Yorkshire Pocket Album
Shropshire
Somerset
South Devon Coast
South Devon Living Memories
South East London
Southampton Pocket Album
Southend Pocket Album

Southport
Southwold to Aldeburgh
Stourbridge Living Memories
Stratford upon Avon
Stroud
Suffolk
Suffolk Pocket Album
Surrey Living Memories
Sussex
Sutton
Swanage and Purbeck
Swansea Pocket Album
Swindon Living Memories
Taunton
Teignmouth
Tenby and Saundersfoot
Tiverton
Torbay
Truro
Uppingham
Villages of Kent
Villages of Surrey
Villages of Sussex Pocket Album
Wakefield and the Five Towns Living Memories
Warrington
Warwick
Warwickshire Pocket Album
Wellingborough Living Memories
Wells
Welsh Castles
West Midlands Pocket Album
West Wiltshire Towns
West Yorkshire
Weston-super-Mare
Weymouth
Widnes and Runcorn
Wiltshire Churches
Wiltshire Living Memories
Wiltshire Pocket Album
Wimborne
Winchester Pocket Album
Windermere
Windsor
Wirral
Wokingham and Bracknell
Woodbridge
Worcester
Worcestershire
Worcestershire Living Memories
Wyre Forest
York Pocket Album
Yorkshire
Yorkshire Coastal Memories
Yorkshire Dales
Yorkshire Revisited

See Frith books on the internet at www.francisfrith.com

FRITH PRODUCTS & SERVICES

Francis Frith would doubtless be pleased to know that the pioneering publishing venture he started in 1860 still continues today. Over a hundred and forty years later, The Francis Frith Collection continues in the same innovative tradition and is now one of the foremost publishers of vintage photographs in the world. Some of the current activities include:

Interior Decoration

Today Frith's photographs can be seen framed and as giant wall murals in thousands of pubs, restaurants, hotels, banks, retail stores and other public buildings throughout the country. In every case they enhance the unique local atmosphere of the places they depict and provide reminders of gentler days in an increasingly busy and frenetic world.

Product Promotions

Frith products are used by many major companies to promote the sales of their own products or to reinforce their own history and heritage. Frith promotions have been used by Hovis bread, Courage beers, Scott's Porage Oats, Colman's mustard, Cadbury's foods, Mellow Birds coffee, Dunhill pipe tobacco, Guinness, and Bulmer's Cider.

Genealogy and Family History

As the interest in family history and roots grows world-wide, more and more people are turning to Frith's photographs of Great Britain for images of the towns, villages and streets where their ancestors lived; and, of course, photographs of the churches and chapels where their ancestors were christened, married and buried are an essential part of every genealogy tree and family album.

Frith Products

All Frith photographs are available Framed or just as Mounted Prints and Posters (size 23 x 16 inches). These may be ordered from the address below. From time to time other products - Address Books, Calendars, Table Mats, etc - are available.

The Internet

Already one hundred thousand Frith photographs can be viewed and purchased on the internet through the Frith websites and a myriad of partner sites.

For more detailed information on Frith companies and products, look at this site:

www.francisfrith.com

See the complete list of Frith Books at:

www.francisfrith.com

This web site is regularly updated with the latest list of publications from The Francis Frith Collection. If you wish to buy books relating to another part of the country that your local bookshop does not stock, you may purchase on-line.

For further information, trade, or author enquiries please contact us at the address below:
The Francis Frith Collection, Frith's Barn, Teffont, Salisbury, Wiltshire, England SP3 5QP.
Tel: +44 (0)1722 716 376 Fax: +44 (0)1722 716 881 Email: sales@francisfrith.co.uk

See Frith books on the internet at www.francisfrith.com

FREE PRINT OF YOUR CHOICE

Mounted Print
Overall size 14 x 11 inches (355 x 280mm)

Choose any Frith photograph in this book.
Simply complete the Voucher opposite and return it with your remittance for £3.50 (to cover postage and handling) and we will print the photograph of your choice in SEPIA (size 11 x 8 inches) and supply it in a cream mount with a burgundy rule line (overall size 14 x 11 inches).
Please note: aerial photographs and photographs with a reference number starting with a "Z" are not Frith photographs and cannot be supplied under this offer. Offer valid for delivery to one UK address only.

PLUS: Order additional Mounted Prints at HALF PRICE - £9.50 each (normally £19.00)
If you would like to order more Frith prints from this book, possibly as gifts for friends and family, you can buy them at half price (with no additional postage and handling costs).

PLUS: Have your Mounted Prints framed
For an extra £18.00 per print you can have your mounted print(s) framed in an elegant polished wood and gilt moulding, overall size 16 x 13 inches (no additional postage and handling required).

IMPORTANT!

These special prices are only available if you use this form to order. You must use the ORIGINAL VOUCHER on this page (no copies permitted). We can only despatch to one UK address. This offer cannot be combined with any other offer.

Send completed Voucher form to:
The Francis Frith Collection, Frith's Barn, Teffont, Salisbury, Wiltshire SP3 5QP

CHOOSE A PHOTOGRAPH FROM THIS BOOK

Voucher for **FREE** and Reduced Price Frith Prints

Please do not photocopy this voucher. Only the original is valid, so please fill it in, cut it out and return it to us with your order.

Picture ref no	Page no	Qty	Mounted @ £9.50	Framed + £18.00	Total Cost £
		1	Free of charge*	£	£
			£9.50	£	£
			£9.50	£	£
			£9.50	£	£
			£9.50	£	£
			£9.50	£	£
Please allow 28 days for delivery. Offer available to one UK address only			* Post & handling		£3.50
			Total Order Cost		£

Title of this book . . . .

I enclose a cheque/postal order for £ . . . .
made payable to 'The Francis Frith Collection'

OR please debit my Mastercard / Visa / Maestro card, details below

Card Number

Issue No (Maestro only)   Valid from (Maestro)

Expires   Signature

Name Mr/Mrs/Ms . . . .
Address . . . .
. . . .
. . . .
. . . . Postcode . . . .
Daytime Tel No . . . .
Email . . . .

Valid to 31/12/12

Can you help us with information about any of the Frith photographs in this book?

We are gradually compiling an historical record for each of the photographs in the Frith archive. It is always fascinating to find out the names of the people shown in the pictures, as well as insights into the shops, buildings and other features depicted.

If you recognize anyone in the photographs in this book, or if you have information not already included in the author's caption, visit the Frith website at: www.francisfrith.com and add your memories.

Our production team

Frith books are produced by a small dedicated team at offices in the converted Grade II listed 18th-century barn at Teffont near Salisbury, illustrated above. Most have worked with The Francis Frith Collection for many years. All have in common one quality: they have a passion for The Francis Frith Collection. The team is constantly expanding, but currently includes:

Paul Baron, Jason Buck, John Buck, Jenny Coles, Heather Crisp, David Davies, Natalie Davis, Isobel Hall, Neil Harvey, Julian Hight, Peter Horne, James Kinnear, Karen Kinnear, Tina Leary, Stuart Login, Sue Molloy, Sarah Roberts, Kate Rotondetto, Eliza Sackett, Terence Sackett, Sandra Sampson, Adrian Sanders, Sandra Sanger, Julia Skinner, Lewis Taylor, Will Tunnicliffe, David Turner and Ricky Williams.